Bear packs her backpack

Castle Mountain

Cats set up camp

Deer and Elk are eating dinner

Emerald Lake, British Columbia

While Fox hides
in the forest

Fernie, British Columbia

H

A Goat
climbs high

Goat's Eye Mountain

Icefields Parkway

We ice skate outside

Jump through juniper trees

Jasper National Park

Lake Louise

**Steal a kiss
on the lake**

Moon over mountains

Middle Sister, Canmore

N

It's nightime in the nest

Lake O'Hara

Owl flies over us

Pika plays peek-a-boo

Peyto Lake

It's quiet in the Rockies

Rundle Mountain

Sunshine Meadows

S **Sheep are sleeping**

T

Trees are tall
above our tent

Temple Mountain

U

Under stars,
night animals
wake up

Upper Hot Springs

The valley has a visitor tonight

V

Valley of the Ten Peaks

**Wind smells
of winter**

Waterton National Park

X marks our favourite spot

X-Country Kananaskis

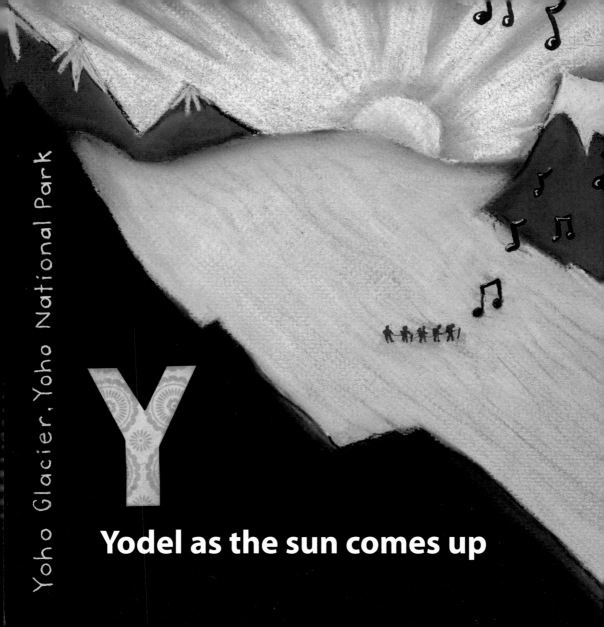

Yoho Glacier, Yoho National Park

Yodel as the sun comes up

And we zoom away.

Grizzly Bowl

RMB | Rocky Mountain Books Ltd.
rmbooks.com
@rmbooks
facebook.com/rmbooks

Cataloguing data available from Library and Archives Canada
ISBN 978-1-77160-163-4 (bound)
ISBN 978-1-77160-500-7 (softcover)
ISBN 978-1-77160-155-9 (electronic)

Design by Chyla Cardinal

Printed and bound in China

Distributed in Canada by Heritage Group Distribution and in the U.S. by Publishers Group West

For information on purchasing bulk quantities of this book, or to obtain media excerpts or invite the author to speak at an event, please visit rmbooks.com and select the "Contact Us" tab.

RMB | Rocky Mountain Books is dedicated to the environment and committed to reducing the destruction of old-growth forests. Our books are produced with respect for the future and consideration for the past.

We acknowledge the financial support of the Government of Canada through the Canada Book Fund and the Canada Council for the Arts, and of the province of British Columbia through the British Columbia Arts Council and the Book Publishing Tax Credit.

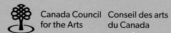
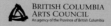